Time for Tea

Time for Tea

A Guide to Tea Rooms
in Leicestershire and Rutland

by Helen Gale

Illustrated by Jacqui Bromley

Kairos Press
1996

First edition, 1996

Design and Layout by Robin Stevenson, Kairos Press.
Body text in Carmina Medium BT 10.5pt.
Imagesetting by CDS Imaging, Leicester,
Printed by Norwood Press, Anstey, Leicester.

Errors And Altered Circumstances

Every reasonable care has been taken to provide up-to-date and accurate information about the establishments featured in this guide. However, tea rooms, like everything else, are subject to changes over time. The details supplied cannot therefore be guaranteed. We recommend that you telephone in advance if you wish to be sure of your refreshment.

No responsibility can be accepted by the author or publisher, for any damages, however caused, resulting from errors, omissions, or information contained in this book.

Kairos Press
552 Bradgate Road
Newtown Linford
Leicester LE6 0HB

Introduction

Writing this guide to tea rooms in Leicestershire and Rutland has been one of the highlights of my life. The only problem is that my bathroom scales keep highlighting a vast weight increase which I hadn't anticipated!

This is very much my personal guide. None of the tea rooms featured have paid to go in the guide. They have all been included on their own merits, as places that appeal to me. Some tea rooms are featured for their character, some for friendly service and value for money, and some because they offer added attractions such as garden or antique/craft centres. By doing this I hope you will find a variety of tea rooms to suit your mood and taste. The symbols at the top of each page may help you in choosing the right tea room (see below).

Leicestershire and Rutland can be very proud of the standard and variety of the tea rooms it offers. I do hope that you enjoy using this guide as much as I have enjoyed writing it.

Helen Gale,
Wigston, 1996

Key to symbols used in this book

 Outdoor seating area.

 Special provision made for children.

 Wheelchair access to the tea room (entire or partial)

 Customer parking is provided

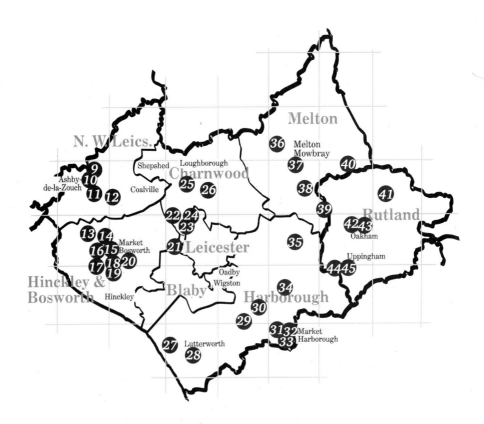

Contents

Map and page No.

16	Bosworth Tea Room, Shenton
17	Whitemoors Antiques & Craft Centre, Shenton
18	The Almshouse, Sutton Cheney
19	Wharf House Tea Room, Sutton Cheney
20	Jasmine Cottage, Cadeby

Blaby

| 21 | Parsons Gallery, Kirby Muxloe |

Charnwood

22	Jade Tearooms, Newtown Linford,
23	Mrs Bouquet's Tea Rooms, Anstey
24	House-e-House Coffee Shop, Anstey
25	Whatoff Lodge Farm Tea Shop, Quorn
26	Stonehurst Farm Tea Shop, Mountsorrel

Harborough

27	Ullesthorpe Garden Centre Tea Rooms, Ullesthorpe
28	Roseanne's Tea Rooms, Lutterworth
29	Jacqui's Tea Room, Saddington
30	Beauchamps, Kibworth Beauchamp
31	Aldin's Tearooms, Market Harborough
32	Joules Eating Place, Market Harborough
33	Aldwinckles, Market Harborough
34	Mill Farm Tea Rooms, Stonton Wyville,
35	Halstead House Farm, Halstead, Tilton-on-the-Hill,

Melton

36	Stonepits Farm Tea Room & Restaurant, Wartnaby
37	Browser's, Melton Mowbray
38	Hollies Farm Tea Room, Little Dalby
39	Gates Nurseries Tea Room, Cold Overton
40	The Windmill Tea Rooms, Wymondham

Rutland

41	Greetham Garden Centre Tea Room, Greetham
42	The Barn at Furley's, Oakham
43	Country Fayre Coffee Shop, Oakham
44	Sweethedges Farm, Stockerston
45	Baines Tea Room, Uppingham

Dedication

To all my family, friends and colleagues who supported me throughout the writing of this book.

Special thanks go to Tony for letting me drive him round umpteen tea rooms! Also Gillian for typing out my illegible notes – you deserve a medal.

Tudor Court Tea Rooms

51a Market Street, Ashby-de-la-Zouch, Leics
Tel: 01530 417610

I'm quite sure Queen Elizabeth I, the famous Tudor Queen, would have approved of this tea room. She may have said to one of her entourage, "Find me a seat in the courtyard my good man. Make sure it is in the shade, so I don't ruin my lily-white complexion."

Opening times:
Mon–Sat: 8.30–4.30.
Sun: 10.30–4.00
Location
Town centre (SK350170)
Market Day: Saturday

Just off High Street, down a little alley, you will find Tudor Court Tea Rooms a welcome watering hole, away from the hustle and bustle of the main thoroughfare. Visitors will discover the menu to be very comprehensive, ranging from breakfasts and cooked lunches, to a set English tea consisting of a selection of sandwiches, a scone with jam and cream, homemade cake, and a pot of tea. Sunday lunches are available till 3.00pm, but you must bring your own wine if you want to indulge in alcohol.

The tea room has ample seating, with two floors laid out with dark wood furniture, and pretty lace tablecloths. In warmer weather you may prefer the sun-kissed courtyard. It might be worth noting that pushchairs and prams are not allowed inside the tea room itself, but naturally these can be accommodated in the courtyard in summer.

Nearby Places to visit:
Ashby Castle
Moira Furnace & Craft Centre (4km, 2m)
Calke Abbey (6km, 3½m)
Donington Motor Racing Museum (10km, 6m)

No. 76, High Street

Ashby-de-la-Zouch, Leics.
Tel. 01530 415901

PARTIAL

Opening times:
Mon–Sat: 8.30–5.00 (early closing, at 4.00pm on Wed).
Location
Town centre (SK350170)
Market Day: Saturday

The only tea room in my book without a name! As I discovered, it doesn't need a name, being a well established tea room and restaurant, popular with both locals and visitors.

I was sorry my visit had to be quite short, as there seemed to be a very mellow atmosphere, condusive to spending an afternoon chatting over tea and cake. The dark wood beams and furniture help create that cosy look, enhanced by rustic farm memorabilia on the walls.

No. 76 specialises in afternoon teas and lunches, Sunday lunch being very popular, so please book in advance. In the summer you can relax in the garden to the rear of the tea room, and enjoy the sun.

If you want to lose yourself in a character tea room then this is the one for you.

Nearby Places to visit:

Ashby Castle
Moira Furnace & Craft Centre (4km, 2m)
Calke Abbey (6km, 3½m)
Donington Motor Racing Museum (10km, 6m)

Staunton Stables Tea Room

The Ferrers Centre, Staunton Harold,
Nr Ashby-de-la-Zouch, Leics. Tel: 01332 864617

I thought I'd died and gone to heaven! They were everywhere – teapots of every shape, colour and size. As a teapot collector, I really felt in my element!

Staunton Harold estate offers so much to see that you'll probably be glad of a chance to sit down with a cup of tea. Whether it's the garden centre, the craft shops or the Sue Ryder charity shop, there's always something to hold your attention. The setting around Staunton Harold is tranquil and beautiful, with lakeside walks waiting to be explored.

Opening times:

Tue–Sun: 10.30–5.00 (close 4.30 in winter) Closed every Monday, except Bank Holidays

Location

5km (3m) north-west of Ashby-de-la-Zouch (SK375215)

The tearoom is part of the Ferrers Centre and in warmer weather most visitors prefer to relax in the stable yard, surrounded by the sun-warmed red brick buildings. Inside is equally pleasant, with pine furniture and vast arrays of teapots and old toys in display cases. A glass-fronted display case reveals scrumptious home-made goodies to be sampled. Light lunches also feature on the menu, including jacket potatoes and toasted sandwiches. Being pro-teapots, I was pleased to see tea is served in a generous sized pot. Tea addicts, this is definitely the place for you!

Nearby Places to visit:

Staunton Harold church & park
Staunton Harold Reservoir
Melbourne Craft Centre (4km, 2m)
Calke Abbey (by foot: 2km, 1m; by road: 5km, 3m)
Moira Furnace & Craft Centre (5km, 3m)
Donington Motor Racing Museum (5km, 3m)

Gardener's Rest Tea Room

Beesley Garden Centre,

Heather Lane Nurseries, Ravenstone, Leics.
Tel 01530 832101

Homemade 'Parsnip and Apple' soup – just the kind of thing you'd expect so see offered in a tea room with this name. As far as I know, Emma, the proprietor, didn't grow them herself, but you never know.

Opening times:

Mon–Sat 9.30–5.30 (closed Wed)
Sun 10.00–1.00

Location

3km (2m) west of Coalville (SK405135)

Nearby Places to visit:

Snibston Discovery Park (2km, 1m)
Donington le Heath Manor House (2½km, 1½m)
Swannington Heritage Trail (2½km, 1½m)

This little tea room is a real oasis. After a long hot drive, I arrived to find people relaxing outside, under a cool canopy. As I sat sipping some refreshing peach-flavoured spring water I thought, "I could stay here all day, drinking in the lovely floral displays around me." Visitors who prefer to sit inside can find a table in the conservatory.

Emma works hard to provide a good range of homemade snacks, cakes and lunches, all priced to offer value for money. A tea room can always be judged by its popularity. The *Gardener's Rest* was very busy. Need I say more?

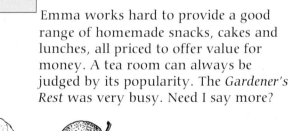

Shackerstone Station Tea Room

Shackerstone Steam Railway Station

Shackerstone, Leics. Tel. 01827 880669

Opening times:

Opening variable, but generally:
Wed & Fri: 12.00–7.00
Sat & Sun: 10.00–7.00

Location

7km (4m) north west of Mkt Bosworth (SK374072)

If you fancy a bit of a change, why not try a visit to the tea room on Shackerstone Station. Don't worry, this won't involve the traditional offerings of the British Rail Buffet! The menu details a wide range of food which knocks the socks off other train travel fare.

The station buildings, dating back to 1873, have been lovingly restored by members of the *Shackerstone Railway Society*. the tea room is housed in part of these, along with a museum and gift shop. Obviously the main attraction is the 'Battlefield Line' itself, with regular train trips available to or from Shenton.

An atmosphere of the bygone era of steam rail travel is perpetuated in the variety of memorabilia in and around the tea room, which used to be the Stationmaster's office. Apparently Edward VII used to alight at Shackerstone when visiting friends at the nearby Gopsall Estate. Knowing Edward's reputation for philandering I can't help wondering if there was a woman involved somewhere!

Nearby Places to visit:

Battlefield Line, Shackerstone Station
Bosworth Water Park (5km, 3m)
Bosworth Battlefield Centre (8km, 5m) (6km, 4m by rail)

Whether it is lunch you want, or just a nice relaxing cup of tea and cake, then Shackerstone Station is well worth visiting.

Manor Farm Tearoom

Carlton Road, Barton-in-the-Beans, Market Bosworth, Leics.
Tel: 01455 290362

Opening times:
Summer: Wed, Sat and Sun: 11.00–5.00 Winter Sat: 11–3; Sun by appointment.
Location
4km (2.5m) north of Mkt Bosworth (SK399064)

Having lived on farms for most of her life, my grandmother always amazed me with stories of how she would regularly prepare Sunday tea for fourteen or more people. Anyone who dropped in uninvited was always welcomed and space was found around the already over-crowded table. "We farmers' wives know how to put on a good spread," she'd say, and I found Betty Jackson's hospitality to be no exception.

The Jacksons have been running Manor Farm for over forty years. Once part of Gopsall Estate, the farmhouse stands on the corner of a quiet cross-roads in the middle of the sleepy village of Barton-on-the-Beans. What have beans got to do with it I hear you ask? Well, the village has developed its own currency, the *Bean!* It's quite a complicated system which probably makes the Single European Currency Mechanism look really easy! However, I hasten to add, Betty requires good old pounds sterling for her afternoon teas.

Whether eating inside the cosy tearoom with its authentic farm house oven and farm-life memorabilia, or relaxing outside in the lovely cottage-style garden under a shady tree, you can be sure of a pleasant visit. Betty's home-made delicacies are enough to make anyone's mouth water. I strongly recommend the 'Afternoon Tea' for value for money and its potential to fill you up! It consists of a toasted teacake with jam or cheese (if you haven't tried Shropshire Blue cheese on a teacake, then prepare yourself for heaven!), a pot of tea that seems to last for ever and a selection of home-made cakes. Betty's Leicestershire Curd Tart is well worth sampling.

There is a warm welcome for everyone at this tearoom. Children are welcome, along with private parties and rambling/cycling club drop-ins. If numbers are above average, give Betty a ring ahead of time. Car parking is also available at the rear of the farm.

The Victorian Tea Parlour

Wheatsheaf Courtyard, Market Bosworth, Leics.
Tel: 01455 290 190

PARTIAL

Standing outside the Police Station at Market Bosworth makes you feel you're on a set for 'Dixon of Dock Green'. This typifies the lovely market town, which maintains its character throughout. Judith and Colin Boam's Victorian Tea Parlour is no exception, so prepare yourself for a truly Victorian experience!

Opening times:
Mon–Sat: 9.00–5.00
(Closed on Sundays)

Location
Village centre
(SK406032)

The Wheatsheaf courtyard is an ideal setting for the tea parlour with a cobbled floor and vibrantly coloured hanging baskets in summer months, the tiny gift shops look most attractive. Stepping into the 'parlour' is just like stepping into someone's front room! Old furniture and Victorian memorabilia give that cosy parlour feel in winter. If you are the outdoor type, then take advantage of the seats in the courtyard. However, in Victorian times, ladies would have been considered 'common' if they had a tan – how times have changed.

Tea is served in traditional brown pottery teapots, oh, save us from the infernal stainless steel pots that always seem to drip!! For the more adventurous, there is a range of speciality teas on offer. Generous portions of home-made fare are served, including cakes, savouries and light lunches.

The tea parlour has a real homely, family atmosphere, with children being well catered for. Despite limited space, wheelchair users can get access.

Nearby Places to visit:
Bosworth Country Park (1km, ½m)
Bosworth Water Park (1½km, 1m)
Bosworth Battlefield Centre (3km, 2m)
Battlefield Line, Shenton Station (3km, 2m)

15

Bosworth Tearoom

Shenton Lane, Market Bosworth, Leics.
Tel. 01455 290144

Breakfast on New Year's Day is just one of the many reasons for visiting the Larkin's tea room. Initially a generous offer after a New Year's Eve party – now a popular Bosworth event! Remember to book in advance to avoid no breakfast.

Opening times:

Sat, Sun & Bank Hol. 10.30–6.00
Weekdays: no set times. Just knock on the door and they'll be happy to serve you.

Location

On SE edge of village (SK404027)

When not serving New Year's breakfasts *Bosworth Tearoom* is equally popular. Serving a range of light snacks on toast, homemade cakes and scones, and cream teas, this lovely old red brick house provides an excellent location. The light, airy conservatory opens out on to a gravel drive shaded by trees to the front. Tables and chairs are set out here in the summer for visitors wishing to dine *al fresco*.

Jean and Tony produce their own honey too (or rather the bees do). So why not take a jar home with you?

Nearby Places to visit:

Bosworth Country Park (1km, ½m)
Bosworth Water Park (1½km, 1m)
Bosworth Battlefield Centre (3km, 2m)
Battlefield line, Shenton Station (3km, 2m)

(The tearoom can also arrange guided walks in and around Bosworth, nature walks, walks around the battlefield, etc.)

Whitemoors Antiques & Craft Centre

Main Street, Shenton, Nr. Market Bosworth, Leics.
Tel: 01455 212 250

Being close to the historic Bosworth Battlefield, it seems fitting that Whitemoors should be offering its own, more recent, items from the past. Apart from tea-rooms, antiques are probably my greatest passion. No wonder my husband confiscated my cheque book!

Opening times:
Wed–Sun, and Bank Hol. Mon: 11.00–5.00
Location
3.5km (2m) SW of Mkt Bosworth (SK385002)

Alongside antique and craft displays, Whitemoors boasts the largest collection of crystal paperweights in the Midlands. As all the buildings are single storey, wheelchair users will find this an ideal place for an outing.

The tearoom is simple yet inviting, with attractive antique wood tables. The light lunches and afternoon teas are all home-made, with tea and cake proving very popular with visitors. The

Nearby Places to visit:
Battlefield line, Shenton
    Station (1km, ½m)
Ashby Canal (1km, ½m)
Bosworth Battlefield Centre
    (2km, 1m)

garden is attractive with the river running through it. They say that on quiet days, if you listen hard enough, you can hear sounds of the Battle of Bosworth drifting across the river.

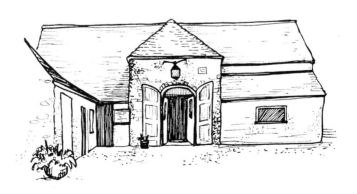

17

The Almshouse

Sutton Cheney, Nr. Market Bosworth, Leics.
Tel: 01455 290 601

Opening times:
Every day: 10.00–5.30

Location
3km (2m) south of Mkt Bosworth (SK416005)

"He erected out of pious mind, an hospital for six poore men, adjoining the church" – so reads the inscription on the tomb of Sir William Roberts. A local Knight, he was known for his good and charitable deeds, including building the Almshouse which now houses the tearoom.

Sutton Cheney village itself is steeped in history. Local legend has it that the church is where Richard III took his last communion before going to his death on Bosworth battlefield. You get a strange sense of timelessness – I kept thinking a knight in shining armour would pop round the corner at any time – no such luck!!

The tearoom is actually situated in the restored stable block. Exposed timbers and tasteful decor help maintain that balance of originality. As in medieval times the food is all home-made. Full lunches are on offer for customers wanting something a little more substantial, but if you just fancy a nice cream tea in the summer, then go no further than the delightful garden terrace – you won't be disappointed.

Nearby Places to visit:
Ashby Canal (1km, ½m)
Bosworth Battlefield Centre (1½km, 1m)
Battlefield Line, Shenton Station (2½km, 1½m)
Bosworth Country Park (3½km, 2m)

Wharf House Tea Room

Sutton Cheney, Nr. Market Bosworth, Leics.
Tel: 01455 212 026

PARTIAL

Wharf House should get a gold star for being child friendly. Philip and Linda Ray have really made an effort to provide facilities for children. The purpose-built outdoor play area means parents can relax outside in the warmer weather and have a cuppa in peace!

Once a pub in the early 1800's called 'The Gate Inn', Wharf house now serves a lighter form of refreshment. The cream tea is good value for money, along with the remaining selection of savouries and cakes.

Opening times:

Tue–Fri: 1.30–5.30
Sat, Sun & Bank Hol.
Mon: 11.30–5.30

Location

Alongside the canal, at Sutton Wharf, 4km (2½m) south of Mkt Bosworth (SK416005)

Being a music lover, I thoroughly enjoyed listening to the beautiful strains of classical music which wafted through the tearoom. My husband had to restrain me from bursting into song!

After downing a slice of fattening cake or a cream tea, take a stroll down to the peaceful Ashby Canal, on the edge of Ambion Wood, and burn up a few calories – you'll need to!

Nearby Places to visit:

Ashby Canal
Bosworth Battlefield Centre (1½km, 1m)
Battlefield Line, Shenton Station (2½km, 1½m)
Bosworth Country Park (3½km, 2m)

Jasmine Cottage

Cadeby, Nr Market Bosworth, Leics.
Tel 01455 291894

Sandra Allen, or *'Jasmine'* to her regular clientele, runs this popular tea room in Cadeby, a little village just outside Market Bosworth.

During my visit I soon realised that people come back time and again to *Jasmine Cottage*, which is an excellent recommendation in itself. As I sampled the menu and general atmosphere of this cosy tea room I soon discovered the secret of its success.

The cottage was built in 1865 by the local churchmen, as a school for the children of Osbaston and Cadeby. Its unusual shape and tiny little windows give it a real quaintness, in keeping with the rest of the village. Inside you get a real cosy parlour feel, especially in winter. In summer the cottage garden proves to be the most popular with visitors. Having visited in winter and summer, I can recommend both.

"All the food on the menu is homemade", says Sandra. "I don't use things from packets." There is always a good range of cakes, pies, savouries and snacks on offer. The gold star has to go to the lemon cheesecake. I knew it was homemade when I came across a small lemon pip – a small sacrifice to make for such a heavenly dessert! If you feel in a lemony mood why not top it off with Sandra's homemade lemonade?

Nearby Places to visit:

Bosworth Country Park (2km, 1m)
Bosworth Battlefield Centre (3km, 1½m)
Battlefield line, Shenton Station (4km, 2½m)

Parsons Gallery

Main Street, Kirby Muxloe, Leicester
Tel: 0116 239 3534

Opening times:
Thur–Sat: 10.00–4.30
Location
6km (4m) west of Leicester, situated just off the roundabout near Kirby Muxloe Castle (SK524048)

If you prefer a relaxing cup of tea without the patter of tiny feet around you, then Parsons Gallery is probably the ideal place! Whilst not being anti-children, the proprietors are keen that children are kept under control due to the vast array of breakable gifts in the shop. It's the kind of shop where parents feel that they need stress relief treatment, or a bank loan when they come out. Needless to say, pushchairs are not allowed in!

With only a few tables in the tearoom, it is often full at weekends. However, on weekdays, it's the perfect setting for a relaxing cup of tea or coffee. All the cakes are home-made and very tasty. The pretty decor of the tearoom is enhanced by a display of prints and originals on the walls. If they don't appeal, then have a wander around the craft shop – there's lots to choose from.

Kirkby Muxloe Castle dates back to 1480 when Lord Hastings began building. Unfortunately his execution cut things a bit short!! Despite its incomplete state, it's still well worth a visit.

Nearby Places to visit:
Kirby Muxloe Castle
Tropical Birdland, Desford (6km, 4m)

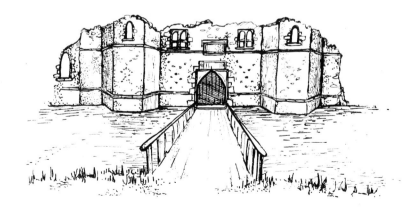

Jade Tearooms

542 Bradgate Road, Newtown Linford, Leics.
Tel: 01530 243664

Opening times:
Mon–Sat: 10.00–5.00(ish)
Sun: 9.00–6.00(ish)
Location
10km (6m) NW of
Leicester (SK521097)

Being a fan of Tudor history, I love visiting Bradgate Park. On weekdays, when it's a little less crowded, I imagine Lady Jane Grey strolling around in the park watching the deer. Such a tragic end to a sweet young girl. I'm sure you're wondering 'what is she rambling on about – this is supposed to be a tearoom guide'! I've always thought it disappointing that there wasn't a really tasteful character tearoom near the park. All those royal connections and no quality tearoom. So you can imagine my delight when Janine and Richard launched 'Jade Tearooms'.

A young couple, with a great deal of hotel experience, Richard and Janine have really put their heart and soul into this tearoom. Whilst pawing over the menu at the counter, I was greeted with the magic phrase "Can I help you madam?"! All their hotel experience has obviously impressed upon the owners the importance of service – if it's good, people want to come back!

The tearoom building is from the late Victorian era and the interior design continues that theme. One picture of Victoria and Albert made me smile – I wonder how many times she'd be saying, silently, "I'm not amused" when boisterous children arrive! However, children are most welcome. The pretty lace tablecloths and framed watercolours go towards creating a relaxing, yet charming tearoom. All home-made, the range of food on offer includes a delicious selection of light lunches such as 'Potato and Stilton Turnovers'. If it's tea and cake you're after, then you won't be disappointed either.

Being opposite the gates to Bradgate Park, it's very convenient to visit after a long walk. The chairs outside mean visitors with dogs are welcome to sit and relax. It may get busy at weekends, but it's well worth a wait.

Nearby Places to visit:
Bradgate Park
Groby Pool (1½km, 1m)
Beacon Hill (5km, 3m)
Great Central Railway,
Rothley Sta. (6½km, 4m)

Mrs Bouquet's Tea Rooms

4 Cropston Road, Anstey, Leics.
Tel: 0116 236 2233

Once inside I thought Patricia Routledge (alias Mrs Bouquet in the TV series 'Keeping up Appearances') would have been proud to be associated with this tearoom. Just the sort of place 'well-to-do' ladies might come for morning coffee!!

Mrs Bouquet's is above the 'World of Flowers' florists, nestled in the very top of the building. Less able visitors and smokers will find two tables specially provided on the ground floor. The main tearoom has a real 'attic' feel, being furnished with antiques and collectables from various eras. Maybe this serves to whet your appetite for the antique gallery adjacent to the tearoom.

Opening times:
Mon–Sat: 10.00–4.30
Closed Sun & Bank Hols
Location
6km (4m) NW of
Leicester (SK553087)

As you would expect (being above a florist!) there are fresh flowers on each table, which compliments the floral crockery. The menu offers a range of cold lunches, savoury and sweet snacks. All the bread and cakes used come from a local bakery. If you like watering your taste-buds with something different, then try one of the specialist teas or coffees. Ordinary tea drinkers will be delighted to find a rising price scale on the cost of pots of tea per person (- no, I'm not trying to blind you with economics!). By ordering a pot for two people, instead of two individual pots, you make a saving – what an excellent idea for people who want a quick cuppa!

After your tea, why not treat yourself to some flowers – you deserve it!

Nearby Places to visit:
Gorse Hill City Farm (2½km, 1½m)
Bradgate Park (3km, 2m)
Swithland Wood (4km, 2½m)
Groby Pool (4½km, 3m)
Great Central Railway, Rothley
   Station (4½km, 3m)

House–e–House Coffee Shop

31 The Nook, Anstey, Leics.
Tel. 0116 236 4400

"What is a Coffee Shop doing in a Tea Room Guide?" I hear you ask. Well it could just as easily be called a tea room as it makes a really good pot of tea!

House–e–House is part of a pine furniture shop of the same name, and as you might expect, the coffee shop is furnished with lovely pine tables and chairs. If you fall in love with the table, you could well take it home with you – or one of the same design, anyway.

Opening times:

Mon–Fri: 8.30–5.30
Sat: 9.00–4.00
Sun: 11.00–4.00

Location

6km (4m) NW of Leicester (SK553087)

The real selling point of the coffee shop is the prices. A range of sandwiches and toasties – mainly ham and cheese with various add-ons – is offered at prices on the whole below £1.00, which I'm sure you will agree gives excellent value for money. There is usually home-made cake available, displayed on the black-board daily, and scones with jam and cream are a permanent feature of the menu. On my visit, the cake of the day was orange cake, which went down well with my cup of tea.

Nearby Places to visit:

Gorse Hill City Farm (2½km, 1½m)
Bradgate Park (3km, 2m)
Swithland Wood (4km, 2½m)
Groby Pool (4½km, 3m)
Great Central Railway, Rothley
  Station (4½km, 3m)

Whatoff Lodge Farm Tea Shop

Woodhouse Road, Quorn,
Nr Loughborough, Leics.
Tel. 01509 412127

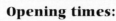

Opening times:
Tue–Sun: approx 10.30–6.00,
mid-March – Sept (closed Mon
except bank hols.) Recommend
phoning to check exact times

Location
4km (2m) south of Lough-
borough, between Quorn and
Woodhouse. (SK547164)

If you like a bit of quirky authenticity then visit Shirley Thomas's tea shop and country walk, down on Whatoff Lodge Farm. Experience everything from pigs, goats, rabbits and lambs, to a strutting territorial cockerel (remember, there's safety in numbers!)

Children will love playing on the climbing frame, and visiting the farm museum, which houses implements and machines used as long ago as 1924. You can even sit down and watch videos explaining every-day farming life. Hey – mums and dads – you may even be able to slip away for a quick cuppa whilst the children are glued to the video.

The tea shop is in the other half of the same barn that houses the museum. Complete with an undulating brick floor (don't worry, I'm sure you won't feel seasick!), pine furniture and whitewashed stone walls, you get a real feeling of being in the country. Cream teas are a speciality, with other cakes and light cold lunches on offer. In the spring months, when it is still a bit chilly, Shirley serves up some of her own home-made soup – a real treat.

If you feel a bit full after your visit to the tea shop, then you could try the country walk. For a small charge you can ramble through one and a quarter miles of lovely Charnwood farmland, abundant with plants and wildlife. Even the odd steam train puts in an appearance, on the Great Central Railway Line which runs through the farm.

Nearby Places to visit:
Great Central Railway, Quorn (½km, ¼m)
Beacon Hill, (3½km, 2m)
Broombriggs Farm Trail (3½km, 2m)
Swithland Wood (4km, 2½m)
Outwoods (5km, 3m)

With so much to see and do here, it's got to be worth a visit.

Stonehurst Farm Tea Shop

PARTIAL

Loughborough Road, Mountsorrel, Leics.
Tel: 01509 413216

My husband tells me I'm too old to visit Farm parks, but I managed to escape with a friend who has a boisterous three-year old. I don't know who had the most fun, him or me! I console myself with the thought that it's very therapeutic to feed baby lambs – well it tickles anyway!

Opening times:
Daily: 10.00–5.00 all year

Location
7km (4m) SE of Loughborough (SK582147)

You can visit the tea shop without visiting or paying for the farm park. There is also an excellent farm shop and museum to visit if you're not a big kid like me! The tea shop is in a converted barn which gives it real character. Lots of lovely cakes and pastries peer temptingly at you through an old display cabinet. In addition to afternoon teas, Marilyn Duffin offers morning coffees and light lunches.

Nearby Places to visit:
Sileby Mill Boat Yard (1km, ½m by foot. 3km, 1½m by road)
Great Central Railway, Rothley (2½km, 1½m) & Quorn (4km, 2½m)
Swithland Wood (5km, 3m)
Broombriggs Farm Trail (6km, 3½m)

Children are especially catered for and birthday parties can be arranged. If you fancy a winter treat, go to the Victorian Christmas evening in December, with donkeys and sheep helping to create a lovely nativity scene.

Ullesthorpe Garden Centre Tea Rooms

Lutterworth Road, Ullesthorpe, Leics.
Tel: 01455 202144

Opening times:
Mon–Sat: 9.00–6.00 (close at 5.00 in winter)
Sun: 10.30–4.30
Location
9km (6m) SE of Hinckley (SP505867)

'Bright, airy and clean' were the first words that came into my head on entering this tearoom. Situated towards the back of the garden centre in a white conservatory with refreshing ceiling fans, the tearoom is the perfect place to relax after a hectic hunt for plants! White metal garden furniture, green gingham tablecloths and a tiled floor, help maintain this aura of cool tranquillity. If you're a sun-lover, then try the sheltered patio and let the trickling pond water be music to your ears.

The menu displays a generous selection of sweet and savoury food. The 'Gardeners' Lunch' offers value for money with ample portions of cold meats, cheese, egg, salad and home-made coleslaw. I have a weakness for lemon cake, so that was my first choice. Due to the large slice I was too full to make a second choice!

Friendly service is always a bonus in a tearoom, but at Ullesthorpe the service was extremely good, both pleasant and informative. I'm sure you'll agree that there's nothing more refreshing than good old British service.

Nearby Places to visit:
Mill-on-the-Soar Falconry Centre (7km, 4m)

27

Roseanne's Tea Rooms

27 Market Street, Lutterworth, Leics.
Tel: 01455 552212

A cup of 'rosie lee' in Roseanne's Tea room is a very worthwhile experience. For starters, the generous pot of tea ensures that you get not just one but two or three cups each! After all that's what tearooms are there for – somewhere to sit and chat over a never-ending pot of tea!

Opening times:
Mon–Sat: 9.00–5.30
Location
Town Centre (SP544845)
Market Day: Thursday

Real child-friendly tearooms are hard to find these days. By that, I mean more than just a highchair and a children's menu. Roseanne's is very popular with families, who love to take advantage of the Family Room upstairs. There are toys, books and a colouring table provided to amuse bored toddlers, who might otherwise seek to get attention in other ways!! Children's parties can be arranged with a resident clown performing tricks.

Downstairs the 'Rose' theme comes across very strongly in the decor and crockery. A wonderful range of teapots are on display (don't worry, Mums, they're on high shelves out of harm's way!).

The usual array of snacks and lunches is on offer daily. My heart was truly warmed on a cold day by a generous portion of home-made treacle tart and custard. It's also worth noting that low fat or fat-free spreads can be used on sandwiches on request – how thoughtful!

Nearby Places to visit:
Stanford Hall (8km, 5m)

Jacqui's Tea Room

Barford House Farm, Mowsley Road, Saddington, Leics.
Tel: 0116 240 2276

Opening times:
Fri–Sun & Bank Hol.
Mon: 11.00–6.00
(closed for July fortnight)

Location
5km (3m) south-west of
Kibworth Harcourt.
(SP658907)

"It's in the middle of nowhere – but you'll find it easily enough!" I was told by a friend, who I suspect didn't get her navigating badge in the Girl Guides! When I reached Jacqui's I realised that was a fair description. (Perhaps she did get that badge after all!) Just take the road out of Saddington sign-posted to Mowsley and you'll find Jacqui's without any problems.

The tearoom is a chalet which looks like it's just been whisked off the set of 'Heidi'! The pine furniture and gingham table cloths give a homespun look, which is equally reflected in the scrumptious food on offer. Whatever your poison (as the saying goes) you're bound to be spoilt for choice by the comprehensive list of home-cooked fare. You can even tuck into a cooked breakfast at teatime if you fancy a winter warmer!

In the summer the gardens provide a haven for weary travellers. Jacqui's ice cream sodas are a must for hot sticky days and even the dogs get bowls of water.

Added attractions at the tearoom are a mini library of second-hand books for sale, and a separate chalet with curios and gifts. Ample car parking is provided, with a closer car park for disabled users.

Nearby Places to visit:
Saddington Resr. (1km, ½m)
Grand Union Canal (2½km, 1½m)
Foxton Locks (6km, 3½m)

Beauchamps

36 High Street, Kibworth Beauchamp, Leics.
Tel: 0116 279 3208

Opening times:
Mon–Fri: 8.30–5.30
Sat: 8.30–5.00
Closed on Sunday

Location
15km (9m) SE of
Leicester, just off
the A6. (SP683937)

What a dilemma! – should I visit the delicatessen first, or the tearoom? Although I was tempted to buy lots of fattening things from the delicatessen, I opted firstly to eat some equally fattening things in the tearoom situated at the rear of the premises.

Beauchamps is a classic tearoom in every sense of the word. There is Classic FM playing in the background, violins on the wall and luxurient furnishings and decor – truly a feast for the eyes. However, the thing that makes a tearoom impressive to me is whether it's a feast for the stomach! I was not disappointed.

Nearby Places to visit:

Grand Union Canal (3km, 2m)
Foxton Locks (5km, 3m)
Wistan le Dale model village,
    Wistow (5km, 3m)
Stoughton Farm Park (9km, 5m)

The menu covers a wide range of cakes, desserts and savouries, including delicious wholemeal toasted teacakes – what a delightful change! The lunchtime menu is changed every day, with a choice of hot or cold food, at very reasonable prices.

With an open fire in the winter and a courtyard garden for summer, Beauchamps is an all-year-round teashop experience not to be missed.

Aldin's Tearooms

PARTIAL

3 Church Square, Market Harborough, Leics.
Tel: 01858 461266

You've heard of the 'traditional corner shop' – well this must fit the bill as the 'traditional corner tea shop'. Aldin's offers a warm welcome to all their customers – including the inquisitive toddler who accompanied me. She would insist on shouting "cuppa tea" at the top of her little voice, but the proprietors were unruffled – even after the twentieth time!

Opening times:

Tue–Sat: 8.45–5.00

Location

Town centre.
(SP734873)

Market Days: Tue, Fri, Sat.

Decorated in pastel colours, the tearoom emits an aura of peace which is a welcome change for any weary shopper. Being located in the centre of this historic market town, Aldins is very handy for a tea-break from a potential 'shop-till-you-drop' outing! The separate floors for smokers and non-smokers allows everyone to enjoy a relaxing cuppa. Whether it's just tea and cake, or a light lunch that you require, you will not be disappointed with the home-made food on offer.

In warmer weather you can relax at the tables on the pavement in front of the tearoom. The beautiful old buildings provide a wonderful setting in which to experience Aldin's food and service.

Joules Eating Place

PARTIAL

*4 High Street, Market Harborough,
Leics.
Tel 01858 462872*

Opening times:
Mon-Sat: 10.00- 5.00 all year
Location
Town centre (SP734873)
Market Days: Tue, Fri, Sat.

"Where's the teashop? – It looks like a dress shop to me, unless they serve tea and cake in the fitting rooms!!" You may well ask this question when searching for Joules Eating Place, but believe me, it does exist! Simply slip down the brick passageway (found to the left of the dress shop) and prepare to be transported back in time.

Originally an old music shop, the tearoom is caught in a 1930's time warp. Art Deco lamps grace the tables, Gerschwin melodies pervade the air and sheet music, dating back to the first war, cover the walls. If you feel in the mood, you could sing for your cuppa! (...groan!). Music Hall memorabilia and a themed display focusing on 'games of chance' all give clues about the proprietors' interests, putting a personal stamp on the tearoom.

On offer is a selection of drinks, home-made cakes and light lunches. All the food is freshly prepared, with an emphasis on healthy eating. Those with a good appetite should definitely try the sandwiches – they really fill you up!

In the summer months you can take tea on the terrace courtyard. Wheelchair access is available to the terrace, but a telephone call in advance would be advisable. High chairs are also provided for small children.

Aldwinckles

PARTIAL

Aldwinckles Yard, 8c Church Street, Market Harborough, Leics.
Tel: 01858 431862

Opening times:
Mon–Sat: 9.00– 5.00
(Closed on Sunday)

Location
Town centre
(SP734873)

Market Days:
Tue, Fri, Sat.

Yet another teashop in Market Harborough tucked away down a small alley. I think Market Harborough should be renamed 'town of the secluded teashops'!

If you're looking for a cosy teashop, especially on cold winter days, then Aldwinckles comes up trumps. Originally a tiny house in an overgrown courtyard, the proprietors have transformed it into a thriving tearoom. With seating available on two floors and courtyard dining in summer, you can usually find a seat.

In winter there is all the ambience of a farmhouse kitchen, reflected in the old brass and copper kitchen utensils. Corn dollies fill the ceiling beams and period photographs of Market Harborough transport you back in time.

Aldwinckles offer a good range of sandwiches, cakes and light cooked meals. The all day 'Breakfast Special' is great for those people who prefer 'brunch' to breakfast. Anyway, who says egg and bacon should be limited to breakfast time?

Wheelchair access to the courtyard would be relatively trouble-free, but due to the petiteness of the tearoom itself manoeuvrability may be difficult. A call in advance would perhaps be advised.

33

Mill Farm Tea Rooms

Mill Farm, Stonton Wyville, Nr. Market Harborough, Leics.
Tel: 01858 545 301

When I think of one word to associate with this tearoom it has to be *'LAMBS'*!! – No, don't worry they won't be sharing your cup of tea with you!

Opening times:
Sat, Sun & Bank Hol. Mon only.
11.00 a.m. – 6.00 p.m.

Location:
8km (5m) north of Mkt. Harborough, 3km (2m) east of Tur Langton. (SP735951)

My first visit to this tearoom was in Spring. Being a working Sheep Farm, the fields immediately surrounding the farmhouse were full of playful young lambs calling to their mothers. A refreshing sight for city dwellers who love to taste a bit of the countryside.

Bill and Diana Sanderson's tearoom has a real feeling of authenticity, from the flagged stone floors, to the whitewashed stone walls. On entering you are greeted with an antique display cabinet full of home-cooked goodies – and Bill ready to take your order. Afternoon teas are their speciality, but they also serve morning coffees and light lunches. The tearoom is ideally located in the middle of the scenic 'Langtons', hence private parties are welcomed by prior arrangement. You could even stay for bed and breakfast if you found yourself taking root there!

Whatever the time of year, I'm sure you will enjoy a visit to this tearoom.

Halstead House Farm

Halstead, Tilton-on-the-Hill, Leics.
Tel: 0116 259 7239

"Oh, please can I go on the tractor and trailer ride?" "No, you can't", replied my husband. "At 31, you're a bit too old for that. Let's settle for the tearoom and nature trail instead – much more sedate for a couple of oldies like us!" However, whether you're old or young, Halstead House Farm and Nature Trail offers something for everyone, including a tearoom well worth a visit.

Opening times:

Easter to end Sept:
daily except mon:12.00–5.30
Sat, Sun, Bank Hols: 10.00–5.30

Location

16km (10m) east of Leicester,
1km (½m) east of Tilton. (off B6047) (SK750057)

An original farm outbuilding has been transformed by David and Susan Driver into a light airy tearoom. Two separate rooms, for smokers and non-smokers, ensures that all customers can relax and enjoy their visit. The stripped pine tables, superb home cooking and friendly service given by Susan Driver all go towards creating that 'down-on-the-farm' feeling. When the warm weather comes the French doors are flung open to give access to a sheltered tea garden, where you will be serenaded by a tumult of melodious bird songs.

Children are well catered for both in the tearoom and on the farm. 'Pond dipping' is one of the most popular activities – so parents, come prepared!! Finally, finish off your visit in the farm shop, for a selection of farm trail souvenirs and fresh farm produce. If you feel like regressing to the medieval era you could even buy a slab of venison to take home – but don't throw the bones over your shoulder!

Nearby Places to visit:

Burough House Gardens (6km, 3½m)
Burough Hill (7km, 4m)

Stonepits Farm

Tea Room & Restaurant

The Salt Way, Wartnaby,
Melton Mowbray. Leics.
Tel: 01664 823 302

A "Nursery Tea for grown-ups"!
– well there's one excellent
reason to visit Stonepits Farm. If
you thoroughly enjoyed eating
your boiled egg and soldiers as a
child, then the 'nursery tea' is
for you! However, that's only
one of a range of afternoon teas to suit all tastes.

Opening times:
Tue–Sun: 11.00–7.00
(last orders 6.00 p.m.)
Closed on Mon except Bank Hols
Location
7km (4m) NW of Melton
Mowbray (SK711231)

The tearoom, consisting of two rooms, has a real 'parlour' feel
about it, with an open log fire, old prints on the walls and various

bits of Victorian china. The high spot is
definitely the food. Ample portions give
you that nice 'podged' feeling, with a
variety of hot and cold food to choose
from. Everything is freshly made, using
free-range eggs. Traditional Leicestershire
fare dominates the menu, including local
Stilton, pork pies and ham, cured to a
closely guarded secret recipe. If you
thought the necessity of secrecy was bad in the leek-growing
fraternity, then you've not talked to ham curers!

The proprietors believe in imposing no restrictions on the timing of
meals. You are welcome to order a pot of tea at lunchtime, a full
breakfast at tea-time and steak & kidney pie for elevenses! – flexibil-
ity is their motto. One exception is the Sunday Roast served between
12 noon – 2.30 p.m. Again,
Stonepits is popular, so order in
advance for lunches.

Nearby Places to visit:
Belvoir Castle (15km, 8m)

Browsers

3 Bowley Court, Sherrard Street, Melton Mowbray, Leics.
Tel: 01664 410085

When I saw the name of this tea room, it conjured up a lovely image in my mind of weary 'window' shoppers sitting with their feet up, enjoying a cup of tea.

Melton is a lovely market town and this tea room proves very popular with shoppers of all ages, but especially pensioners. Why? (I hear you ask.) Do they provide couches for these weary pensioners to rest on?

| **Opening times:** |
| Mon-Sat: 9.30–5.00 |
| Closed Sundays. |
| **Location** |
| Town centre (SK755190) |
| **Market Days:** Tue, Sat. |

No – the answer is excellent home-cooked food at very reasonable prices. I'm sure you'll agree that's a plus point for everyone. We British like to get value for money.

The 'Specials' board is always host to a variety of tempting delicacies, in addition to the good selection of savoury snacks and cakes. There is nothing I find more disappointing than 'plastic' tasting lemon meringue!! At Browsers you get the real thing, topped off with a glass of homemade lemonade if you fancy.

The No-Smoking policy between 12.00 and 2.00, and the friendly service all help towards making Browsers well worth a visit.

Hollies Farm

Tea Room and Craft Centre

Little Dalby, Melton Mowbray, Leics. Tel: 01664 454553

Antiques are one of my passions. It's just a shame that in most cases my passion exceeds my pocket! The tearoom at Hollies Farm sits amidst a craft and antique display, so it enabled me to enjoy both my passions simultaneously.

Various farm outbuildings house the craft centre, with the tearoom situated in a barn conversion. In warm weather the tables in the cobbled stable yard are very popular, whilst some visitors favour the cool stone-walled tearoom.

Opening times:
Sat, Sun and Bank Hols: 11.00–4.30 (Closed between Christmas and Easter)
Location
7km (5m) south of Melton, 11km (7m) NW of Oakham (SK775140)

The menu is restricted mainly to cakes, pastries and savouries, but what it lacks in variety, it certainly makes up for in quality. All home-made, the cakes are positively scrumptious and can be washed down by a refreshing cup of their speciality tea.

Being in the next room, the antique and craft display provides a pleasant distraction, allowing you to wander round and come back to enjoy that all important second cup of tea.

Little Dalby is a delightful village, nestled deep in the countryside between Oakham and Melton. A perfect destination for a relaxing country drive.

Nearby Places to visit:
Burough Hill (3km, 1½m by foot. 5½km, 3m by road)
Burough House Gardens (5km, 3m)
Rutland Railway Museum, Cottesmore (13km, 8m)

Gates Nurseries Tea Room

Somerby Road, Cold Overton, Leics. Tel: 01664 454 309

During my research for this book I began to realise that tearooms and garden centres seem to go together rather well. That set me thinking – tea and gardening go together rather well at our home too. My husband gardens and I drink the tea!

Opening times:

Mon–Fri: 10.00–5.00
Sat, Sun & Bank Hols: 10.00– 5.30
Jan–Mar: close at 4.30

Location

6km (4m) NW of Oakham (SK810104)

Gates Nurseries Tea Room was a firm favourite for inclusion in my tearoom guide right from the start. Cold Overton is a timeless village in the heart of the countryside. The breath-taking scenery alone puts you on an emotional high. Then a walk through the well laid out nurseries brings you to the tearoom, which I found to be equally scenic!

Beamed ceilings, a stone flagged floor, pine furniture and tasteful print curtains help create a real country ambience. Even when full, the spaciousness of the room prevents that over-crowded feeling. Hours could have been spent just looking at the lovely pictures and prints for sale on the walls.

In today's society value for money is important, especially if you have children. A visit to some teashops can almost cost an arm and a leg! At Gates Nurseries value for money is a high priority. The freshly made soup, savouries and cakes were very reasonably priced but, most importantly, the pot of tea was **large**. You don't need to spend time arguing over who's having a second cup! If you're a tea fanatic, try their large range of speciality and iced teas – well worth it!

Nearby Places to visit:
Burough House Gardens (6km, 4m)
Burough Hill (5km, 3m)
Rutland Water (8km, 5m)

The Windmill Tea Rooms

Wymondham Windmill, Butt Lane,
Wymondham, Leics. Tel: 01572 787 304

This is the only tea room I've visited that organises a reception committee for visitors. It consists of chickens, ducks, and a Vietnamese po t-bellied pig! However, after a while you realise that it isn't just because they're pleased to see you, they also hope you're going to feed them. If another car arrives, you'll soon see where their loyalty lies – bread!

Opening times:

Tue–Sun and Bank Holiday Mons: 10.00–5.30
(Nov–Feb: weekends only)

Location

10km (6m) east of Melton, 11k (7m) north of Oakham (SK850193)

Vincent Manchester runs a lovely tea room, getting up at some unearthly hour to bake all the cakes, etc., for that day – now there's dedication for you! First prize goes to his 'toffee fudge cake'. It's just like eating six melt-in-the-mouth pieces of toffee fudge in one go – you can't beat it. A close second are the range of home-made soups on offer at lunchtime, nice and filling for a mid-day snack. Luscious cream teas are a speciality, with diabetic jams available.

Children will love this tearoom as they get their own special mugs designed to avoid spillages. Afterwards they can visit the animals and try their hand at the 'Little Devils' rally karts in warmer weather. Grown-ups don't miss out either as there are plenty of craft and antique shops to look around in the complex next to the tearoom

The windmill is being lovingly restored to its former glory. Adults and older children will find it well worth exploring.

Nearby Places to visit:

Rutland Railway Museum, Cottesmore (8km, 5m)
Rutland Open Air Theatre, Tolthorpe Hall (12km, 7m)
Clipsham Yew Tree Avenue (13km, 8m)

Greetham Garden Centre Tea Room

Oakham Road, Greetham, Rutland
Tel: 01572 813 100

Opening times:
All year, 7 days a week: 9.00–5.00
Location
8km (5m) NE of Oakham (SK925144)

Cat lovers will be at home in the Garden Centre, as David Penny's cats are definitely part of the fixtures. Despite being very sociable cats, they know their place. You will not find them begging in the tearoom, you're more likely to find them curled up in a nice warm box on one of the shelves – wise cats!

Kitted out with garden furniture (naturally!) the tearoom is a new addition to the Garden Centre. Whilst not boasting a character appearance, friendly service and value for money make up for all that. There are very few tearooms where you can purchase tea and cake for two and still have change from £2! The home-made cakes are scrumptious – particularly the ginger and banana cake with lemon icing – what a combination!

Nearby Places to visit:

Rutland Railway Museum, Cottesmore (3km, 2m)
Clipsham Yew Tree Avenue (5km, 3m)
Rutland Water (7km, 4m)
Rutland Open Air Theatre, Tolthorpe Hall (12km, 7m)

Additional attractions, like a children's playground and a falconry centre offer a worthwhile visit for families. The kids can play while mum and dad choose some new plants! If you've got gardening queries – David's your man. Watch out Alan Titchmarsh, you may have a rival!

41

The Barn at Furley's

P

12 Burley Road, Oakham, Rutland
Tel: 01572 770245

A paradise for hayfever sufferers – you get flowers on the table, but they're hand-knitted!! One of the many pleasant surprises you will find on a visit to *Furley's*.

The menu offers a veritable feast. Being a Stilton fan I had to sample the Stilton and celery scones with an additional wedge of Stilton on the side. I'm sure a diet will be high on my list of priorities after researching this book! Lunches are served between noon and 2.30 p.m. with a wide selection of carefully thought out dishes to choose from. Try the home-made cakes – you can even buy some to take home. The speciality teas and coffees should not be missed either.

Surrounded by the luxuriously tasteful decor, visitors will soon realise that *Furley's* is an upmarket tearoom and this is reflected in the prices. However, all things being considered, it's well worth the money – so go on, treat yourself.

Nearby Places to visit:
Oakham Castle (½km, ¼m)
Rutland Water (3km, 2m)

Country Fayre Coffee Shop

6 Crown Walk, High Street, Oakham, Rutland.
Tel. 01572 724504

Oakham being a lovely rural market town in the heart of Rutland, it seemed fitting to see a quaint little watering hole called *Country Fayre*.

Tucked away down at the bottom of a little glass-covered arcade of shops, the 'coffee shop' (which also serves tea – of course) is very cosy. The lower half of the windows are covered with pretty café curtains, to give that all important feeling of seclusion. Decorations such as original watercolours of local scenes, and a collection of old plates, all help to create a country ambience.

Opening times:
Mon–Sat: 9.30–4.30
Closed on Sundays
Location
Town centre (SK861089)
Market Days: Wed. & Sat.

Breakfasts are served till 3.00pm, but if you feel in need of a well earned lunch break during a hectic shopping trip, then the selection of filled baguettes on the daily specials board could be just the ticket. During winter months, try one of their range of oven-baked dishes, to be found under the 'hot pots' section of the menu. (But don't worry, you won't need oven gloves to handle them!) With cold and hot desserts to choose from, and friendly service, you'll soon put *Country Fayre* on your list of regular haunts.

Nearby Places to visit:
Oakham Castle (½km, ¼m) Rutland Water (3km, 2m)

Sweethedges Farm

Allexton Road,Stockerston, Rutland
Tel: 01572 717 398

'Off-the-beaten-track' would best describe this tearoom – but don't be put off or you'll miss out on friendly service, home-made cakes and a lovely beauty spot. If unsure of the location, Brian and Anita Bray will always be very glad to give you directions.

Opening times:
Every day except Tue:
10.00–6.00 (Open all year)
Location
Mid way between Stockerston & Allexton. 4km (2m) west of Uppingham (SP827994)

Food isn't the only thing that makes a tearoom good. Service is equally important. Brian made me feel most welcome, taking time out to describe the various country walks around the tearoom. Whilst sipping the tea you can simultaneously drink in the rolling hills, woods and meadows. Due to a long-term commitment to conservation on the farm, you can see a profusion of wildlife throughout the year – a delight for children and adults alike.

Nearby Places to visit:
Hallaton Village Museum (6km, 4m)

If casting a line and landing a few fish is your passion, then why not make a day of it and relax by the lake, well-stocked with fresh-water fish. Permits can be obtained on site.

Sweethedges Farm is also very popular for lunches. Being open all year round, they have built up a regular clientele, so advance lunch bookings may be advisable. Whether it's morning coffee, lunch or afternoon tea, Sweethedges will always come up trumps!

Baines Tea Room

5 High Street West, Uppingham, Rutland
Tel (01572) 823317

Opening times:

Mon–Sat: 9.00–5.00 (last orders 4.45) Closed Sun & Bank Holidays.

Location

Town centre (SP855998)

Market Day: Wed.

Despite being a very up-market small town, famed for its private school, you could not get a more friendly, down-to-earth service. Peg and Jean welcome you to their tea room in a building which dates back to the 17th century, although it has only been used as a tea room since 1965.

Being in the heart of Uppingham, the window seats provide an excellent vantage point. You really can watch the world go by, whilst sampling some of the delicious home-cooked fare on the menu. Highly recommended is the home-made soup, served with rolls fresh from the bakers next door. For a lighter afternoon snack try the flapjack. However don't be deceived by the size of the piece, one slice may well fill you up.

The homemade food, original features, and friendly service combine to make Baines Tea Room well worth a visit.

Local History and Natural History in Leicestershire and Rutland

with Kairos Press

The following books are available in bookshops throughout Leicestershire and Rutland, or post-free at the prices shown, from Kairos Press
552 Bradgate Road, Newtown Linford, Leicestershire LE6 0HB

BRADGATE PARK
Childhood Home of Lady Jane Grey.
Joan Stevenson & Anthony Squires

ISBN 1-871344-02-6 (1994) 60 pages, 30 pictures, 3 maps.

£3.50

For over five centuries the history of this well loved beauty spot was inextricably bound up with the fortunes of the Grey family, before the park was given to the people of Leicestershire in 1928. This book narrates that history, along with accounts of the landscape, deer, former village of Bradgate, the ruins, and the present day park.

"An admirable booklet ... it will appeal to all who have an affection for Leicestershire and its history" — VILLAGE VOICE

A Family Guide to
CHARNWOOD FOREST.
Joan Stevenson

ISBN 0-905837-04-5 (1982) 56 pages, 33 photographs. *£2.50*

'A highland landscape in miniature', Charnwood has some of the best loved sites in Leicestershire. Its history, landscape and people are here vividly portrayed.

Leicestershire and Rutland
WOODLANDS
Past and Present.
Anthony Squires and Michael Jeeves

ISBN 1-871344-03-4 (1994)160 pages, 54 pictures, 29 maps. **£9.95**

An excellent, detailed account of how woodlands in the two counties have evolved and been managed since before Roman times. Wildlife, present day management, and classification of woodlands are described, and there is a series of case studies on specific woodland sites.
"Readers will see our local woodland heritage in a new light. I strongly recommend it to all those with an interest in the countryside."
— DEREK LOTT, OF LEICESTERSHIRE MUSEUMS.

Memories of
NEWTOWN LINFORD.
edited by Joan Stevenson

ISBN 1-871344-04-2 (1994) 64 pages, 37 photographs. **£3.50**

Newtown Linford was owned by the Grey family until the 1920s, and the book records the fascinating memories of a group of villagers – church; school; work; day trippers; life at the Victorian Bradgate House; and the upheaval when the estate was sold.

LEICESTER THROUGH THE AGES.
Joan Stevenson

ISBN 1-871344-05-0 (1995) 108 pages,
59 photographs, 6 engravings, 6 maps.

£5.50

From its beginnings before the Romans arrived,
Leicester's history is traced through Roman, Danish and Medieval times, civil strife, and industrial expansion, to give a lively and vivid picture of the background to the present day city.
"The best ever written about Leicester ... I just could not put it down."
— ERIC SNOW, HISTORIAN

Index

Time for Tea

Tea rooms featured in this guide

From remote rural retreats in rolling countryside to secluded corners of bustling market towns — Leicestershire and Rutland have a delightful array of tea rooms, to suit all tastes and satisfy the thirstiest tea drinker. Helen Gale has selected 37 of her favourites, for inclusion in this guide, so that when it's time for tea you can find just the place you are looking for.

Kairos Press

ISBN 1-871344-08-

9 781871 344080